COURAGE AND GRIT:A PHYSICIAN'S JOURNEY FOR HEALING AGAINST ALL ODDS

Dr. Smita Kittur

INTRODUCTION

My husband, a transplant surgeon, ended up receiving a double lung transplant for a fatal condition called pulmonary fibrosis. He survived the illness. Due to immuno-suppression needed to keep the lungs alive, he developed a brain infection called Progressive Multifocal Leukoencephalopathy (PML) where he lost his ability to speak and cognize. As there is no treatment available for PML, he was informed to join hospice.

The book is about the courage and grit it took to navigate the medical system, explore experimental treatments for potential cure.

The book is a collection of journal notes from the daily diary. It discusses the spiritual tools I used to strenghten my psychological health but during the process, I discovered the love for my husband, intesified in life without words

Silent Love

"Words, words, words"..... Shakespeare moaned futility of words in Hamlet and continued to complete the play in more words.

Words are all I have to record my Silent Love, my experience of courage, grit and spirituality.

Here they are......

Dr. Smita Kittur

Contents

1.   ABSENCE OF WORDS

You came to pick me up at the Ladies' Hostel on Sunday at 4pm in the second year of our medical school.

The first time we were going out.

My shyness swallowed all my words like a crocodile. You got caught up in the net of my lack of words.

To escape this trap, you held my hand and asked me gingerly, "Tell me, what are the thoughts holding your words, hostage in your mind?" Lacking words, we sat in the front seat of a 4 limited double-decker bus on the top floor. Touched for the first time, the two got dragged into the waterfall of new emotions and began to like the lack of words.

When we reached Juhu Beach, we were sitting in front of the wall in an isolated spot. Our first kiss prevented the words from coming out. But as the exam approached, the rapid fire of question answers began the word duel. Those words had to come out as if the house was on fire.

America, the world, name, fame, patients, friends, mother, and children all shared your words. I started missing your words. Because of all the responsibility, my words began to shoot on sight as needed. Most of all, to complain to you.

Illness retired you. My competition for words with workers ceased. I started enjoying more and more of your words. Competition was now all about friends, travel, and hobbies.

Vipassana says to observe silence, to attain enlightenment, but we cannot remain silent. Those words were squirming inside, crying to come out. We left the intention of silence and enlightenment for the next birth.

Until one day, words decided not to wait for the next birth. They sat inside you with the help of brain lesions. The complete absence of your words in three days made my thoughts numb.

Slowly life began without words. Vipassana silence started showing its benefits.

Friends, parties, and travel are all gone. Only you and I left for each other just as we first met in medical school. Needless to say; If you say M, I understand Mountain Dew. I understood that most of our talking used to be about the world. After living together for 48 years, words are not needed to communicate.

You try to talk, to teach me how to be alone when you're gone. Leave it to your Dutta, your favorite god; he is there to take care of me. Talking about worldly things seems to be talking nonsense now. How close I feel to you without words.

Today I understand for the world, you need a flow of words, but for love, you need the absence of words!

2.   LIFE IS A RIVER

Yesterday was day 7 of your infusion. You woke up, didn't hug me, you were quiet. "Dubs- are you ok?" I asked. You tried to speak, but the words were heavy like lead. Like I was watching a slow-motion movie, the words were coming out at a turtle's pace, as if the words had forgotten their own personality.

I could see and feel the fear in your eyes. I had told God I would accept whatever was given to me. But how far do you want to stretch me, God? How hard do you want this test to be?

Was Aphasia not enough that now you want to insert confusion into his calm delicate mind? All the courage I had collected through spiritual practices collapsed like a house of cards. My mental weakness scared me like a Devil.

I started doubting if I could come out of this storm alive without drowning? Is my mind strong enough? No one is here with me. I feel so alone. But why do I need someone? Why am I feeling so weak? Where did the faith go in me and in God?

I read this morning. When can I get good thoughts and words? When I do not need the support of the outside world. When you lose the dependence on the outside world. Once you lose that dependence, the fear goes. That is when you express yourself.

Joy and strength. I decided then at that stage, why can't I be that? Why do I need pity from other people to prop me up psychologically, like the house of Cards? I will rather be strong like the concrete foundation of the house.

Today's meditation helped too. Visualize you are standing at the bank of the river. Life is flowing like water in the river. Flowers deadwood all. But I am steady and strong, watching the life flow.

Today MD Anderson accepted you for their clinical trial. A ray of hope is shining through my mind. But I am watching that too from the bank of the river. All this is happening in the river, and I am not getting wet, getting carried away. I am standing strong at the bank, watching my life flow.

Watching the sky, feeling free.

That is freedom.

3. MY MENTAL TORNADO

Last night, your tube feed showed its might. However hard I tried to push, the block in your tube stood like a loyal security guard and emphatically refused to let the tube feed enter your stomach. Tug of war went on between my push and your tube's resistance.

After looking at the suffering on your face, I finally surrendered. That tube refused to let you eat that night. Your stomach was hungry for food and my mind for peace. Both slept hungry.

Being a doctor and not being able to help you shattered my ego into pieces and merged into the dust at the bottom of the cliff. Then the storm arose in my mind, slowly picking up the speed of the full-blown tornado.

The only thread of hope I was holding onto was the chance for you to be in an experimental trial at Houston. The dark thoughts and fear twisted in my mind and shredded my intellect as if passed through a grinder into unrecognizable small pieces.

How many pieces? Did I do everything right? Should I have taken you to the emergency room last night? What if you contracted Covid in the emergency room while waiting there for hours for your treatment?

Because the Interventional radiologist placed the tube in you, the gastroenterologist wouldn't see you. The other doctor's treat you as untouchable if the competitors gave you the treatment. How will you be able to travel to Houston for your experimental treatment with a blocked tube, making you unable to feed traveling 8 hours with no nutrition.

If you don't get the chance to get into the clinical trial on time, the disease is rapidly progressing, the death is guaranteed. How will I get out of this tornado? They say if you stay in the eye of the tornado, you can survive. I need to find the eye of my mental tornado. Fortunately, found it in today's meditation.

The world is a projection of the mind. What does that mean? I wondered. People are there, but the relationships are projections. You are my husband, and my best friend is a projection. I decided to drop the baggage of mind. So, I looked at you just as my patient. What would I do as a doctor in this situation? Logic started flowing in. See the facts. Do this, do that. Why, then was there such a storm of emotions? My mind was slowly getting under my control.

Without any fear, I tried hot water, a lot of coke pushing in your tube. This time I won. The block dissolved. You got your feed. The storm in my mind

subsided. I realized holding on to the attachment to the relationship as my husband created the tornado.

And loosening that attachment gets you out of the mental tornado. I feel good now. I feel the peace in my mind. You got your food, and I got my peace. Both were happy fulfilling our different needs!

4.   A,B,C,D,E,F,G

Last night, I saw you sitting on the family room sofa, with your legs stretched, holding the remote control, intently focused on the TV, rocking your head, left and right, up and down, singing along A,B,C,D,E,F,G. How innocent, how cute you looked. Your green eyes were following and dancing along with your neck with the letters A.B.C.D.E.F.G on TV.

How proud I am of you, how enthusiastically you are doing speech therapy. Those words were your friends for the last 70 years, but now they are acting like a two-year-old boy scared to come out of your head. One or two will pop out like popcorn, but when you listen to this song on TV, one after the other, they line up and flow out of your head, saying A,B,C,D,E,F,G!

Suddenly, my admiration for you is replaced by my pity. One-time well-renowned transplant surgeon. your famous lectures, your 100+ publications, now is watching kindergarten songs to learn A,B,Cs. I felt a knot in my stomach; I felt like someone squeezed my heart through a wringer cycle of a washer.

Tears in my eyes wanted to come out at high speed, but then I remembered the promise you made me give to you three weeks ago. You said, "If I stop talking, please don't have pity on me" You were crying, and I made you the promise I will not have pity on you. I did not let that red light signal turn green for those tears; alas, they reversed back into my heart.

With a smile on my face, I started singing along with you, A,B,C,D,E,F,G. I hugged you hard, and we started dancing at the song: A,B,C,D,E,F,G. In the background, on TV, was the dance of the children, and we were doing our fox trot. It reminded me of the dance we did at your department of surgery Christmas gala when you sang Strangers in the Night, pulled me from the audience, and started dancing. How everyone was admiring your courage! The circumstances are different, but the joy is the same.

I am realizing today happiness is not outside but is in mind. You can summon it any time on demand, just sing A,B,C,D,E,F,G !

5.   INTENSE LOVE

Your illness propelled us towards partial renunciation. First lost our careers, then travels, then friends and family. Just two of us left, in our world, you and me, meant for each other. Slowly, the other senses' attractions started abating; how many times god must have asked us to let go, but we couldn't do.

But the letting go happened when you lost your speech and eyesight. There were no desires left. Knowing you were so close to death, your guru asked you to tell her one desire you want to fulfill. You said you had none. Just a small attachment is left for Smita. What will happen to her after I die.

She told you not to worry about me. She will take care of me. She will move me to Florida, and she will always watch over me. You were content knowing someone was there to take care of me. We both have become like monks. We don't have any worldly desires. I didn't know if you let go of material things, you would get a thousandfold more love in return!

All your focus is on me, and mine on yours. Just as when young boy and girl meet for the first time, how happy they are and smile at each other. Whenever we cross each other in the house, we don't move without a kiss and a hug. We have no complaints about each other. Your disability has become the ability of our love.

We walk every day for 2 1/2 miles, listening to Digambara, om namo bhagavate Vasudeva, and Shivohum, 20 minutes each. We hold each other's hands when we walk because you can't see, but I let the people feel and think what they want to. They think we are a romantic couple.

You can't talk, but you know things. You somehow communicate with me. When we talk about your medical care, and we have to make so many new decisions about your care daily, you have assigned one doctor to each finger. The Thumb means Dr. Tokman, the Middle finger for Dr. Grimley in Cincinnati, and the ring finger for Dr. Olsen at MD Anderson. I am learning grit from you. You will not give up your charade until I get the point, way beyond my patience, but when I finally get it, we laugh so much as if we won a game.

Just each other's presence pours so much intense love I don't think people will understand it. This is like spiritual love. Today I realize that after letting go of worldly pleasures after the outside disturbance subsides, Pure love remains, intense love, and peace!

6.   RISE ABOVE

You and I are passing through these gutter pipes of your illness. Inside this gutter is garbage, smell, stones. We are being thrown in this current, banging on the walls from left to right and right to left. But don't give up courage. Don't give up hope even if the doctor says you have six months to live. I promise you we will get out of this gutter pipe at the end.

Swami TV said today, don't tolerate pain; endure it. Endure both pain and pleasure equally.

We are holding each other's hand through this journey of life, sometimes good, sometimes bad, but most importantly, we are making the journey holding each other's hands, so let us enjoy it. Let us pretend your illness is the Disney land roller coaster ride; we will be afraid while going up but will have fun going down. Just hold on.

Gayatri was saying, swami said to have 3 beakers with 4, 25, and 60 degrees temperature water. One is cold like ice, the other normal, and the third very hot. Put 2 fingers in cold and hot water each, endure the pain, and now put all four fingers in normal water. All fingers will feel better. Increase your endurance.

We have a chance to increase our endurance through your disease. Let us not complain. Let us endure. As

we increase our endurance, we will not feel the pain. How the knowledge appears at the right time. Does it make you believe in some superpower taking care of us?

All around us is intelligence, but the pain and pleasure are in the mind. It is a wave in the consciousness; it comes and goes. You just witness it. The pain is not real. It is a wave of mind. The waves occur in Hiranyagarbha. I don't know if you will understand this.   But with this endurance, rise above this pain and pleasure.

Do not identifying with the pain. It is a movement in mind; it is not real. Now rise above and see the whole picture. Your increasing worry about your continuing loss of function, and what will happen to me are all in your mind. They are not real. Do not identify with them.

Let us both hold our hands and fly above in the higher consciousness, watching our life, enjoying forever!

7.   LOST AND FOUND

D day was yesterday

The T cells enter your body

The waiting starts! Tick tick tick

The cells will either win and kill the virus sparing your life, or die themselves and take your life.

You won't know until 2 weeks.

The virus dies, or you die slowly for both.

Waiting period how do I fill the time? Especially for my mind. The mind is squirting out thoughts of hope in all directions like a sparkler when lit.

I imagine you're well and back to normal speaking, eating, traveling, and enjoying life.

Many castles are built in my mind; what will I do when I get better.

But then, like someone poured water on that lit sparkler, the water of fear dissolves all my hopes.

What if it doesn't work? What will be life? Now the mind is caught in the current of negative thoughts. How will your disease progress? How much will you suffer?

Will I have the strength to endure? Will helplessness rule over me? Will you lose your mind, get paralyzed, or will you aspirate? I can't even imagine.

Today's meditation is coming to my rescue. When the person is flowing in thoughts, he is lost in the world. I see myself getting lost.

But when you stop thinking, stop flowing in the river, and watch yourself, suddenly, the mind is quiet. Peaceful, you find yourself.

I realized I was getting lost in the world and coming back to myself,

I feel peace.

He said just be.

Not what next, just be.

By being, you will be able to see yourself.

So much peace.

Glad I found myself after being lost in those thoughts and that world.

At least for today or some time, I have the peace.

I know that mind will come back with a vengeance tomorrow; I will deal with it then. Let me enjoy the peace I found today.

8.   SHAKE OFF YOUR UNHAPPINESS

Engaged in my own problems

lost in my own darkness

feeling sorry for myself

blaming others for not helping

These thoughts want to pop out

They want to drown me and

dominate my psyche

But wait. I have a flashlight

That shines a light on those dark thoughts

you can't survive in this house

As soon as I shine a light on you

You will run away like cockroaches

Swami's meditation led me to see my body,

legs and bones as earth

The abdomen and all organs as water

The stomach as fire

The lungs as air

And the head has Aakasha, the ether

Now I am just a stack of all these 5 elements

Are they universal or personal?

Of course, universal.

But when I see it as personal,

The insecurity and fear set in

I see myself as limited

Despite the full power of all

But underneath all, I am the unlimited power.

I just need to shake off the ignorance that I am separate from
this universal power

Once I access myself by shedding the ignorance, everything I
think

happens, so watch your mind

If you think negatively, it is going to happen, but when I watch
my thoughts, my actions

and realize if they are from a limited source or worldly, not
mine, they disappear and

I enter my universal self,

the universal power

like shake off the unhappiness

you, you are already happy

I shall practice this

Remind me who I am and all that insecurity and fear is not
mine. Let me abide in myself that

by shedding off this separateness, this

ignorance and discover

I am fearless and desireless. What I think happens, why will I then be thinking

Negative?

My flashlight is on, looking for those cockroaches, fear, anger, jealousy and blame

As they run away, I start seeing the peace, strength, and happiness in me.

9.   **A SEARCH OF WHO AM I**

Swami TV's meditation came to the rescue.
So, I am determined to be myself
What am I? Who am I? Look at yourself.
What you think who you are as a person made up of all
    identifications, mind, and body that is not you
To find yourself, you have to dismantle this mental person
    piece by piece

that can be done
make that person impersonal
Drop that me and mine,
Nothing is mine, and all is mine. I am aware of everything,
    but it is not mine.
Now see that person with none of these identifications
you are not any of the roles you are playing

once the identification is dropped
Pure awareness arises, storms in mind stop
Pain, pleasure stop
Happiness, Joy peace enter
Now that I know who I am not supposed to be and who I
    am supposed to dismantle, my journey begins today.

10.   SPEECH RIDE

I wrote the sentence, Jim
wanted you to learn
the quick brown fox jumps over
the lazy dog, which has all 26 syllables
I know you don't give up
So, I made you repeat after me

Each word in the sentence waiting
to see how many turns it will take
for you to learn
100 repetitions. Both you and I continued
But your brain refused to catch it
Convinced I was this approach is not working
So I am on the internet searching for Aphasia treatments

I have decided to take over this speech therapy.
Talking devices for Aphasia, speech generating devices
    for Aphasia,
sentence software for Aphasia
Email for Aphasia There is hope.
Brain fitness, and brain training apps look for an apps
    for Apple, symbol or print-based, responding to speech
    input, and does it provide spoken output?

Talking about apps for Aphasia,

constant therapy based on brain plasticity with 75 task-
    based categories, 100000 exercises $ 25 a month stroke
    approved.

Lingraphica has a laptop model

All talk and tablet model Touch Talk and Minnie Talk
    17 voices, email and instant messaging, insurance

reimbursable, app is small talk that is free for practicing speech.

Lingraphica's talkpath therapy has 11,500 speech languages and cognitive therapy

Free from web or talk path therapy, app free

Prologue 250 for people who have difficulty speaking or cannot speak et al. It uses symbols Costs $219.99 tactnotherapy.com / find 5 to 25 $

 no wi-fi needed

Tapgram -tap share connect gets posted on your social media free on phone, tablet and if you make an app send to naa@apphasia.org

So much to explore

But I will do it and find you the right app. We will ask for a new speech therapist today.

Think of it as a new roller coaster ride called the speech ride. Let's hold our hands and enjoy the ride.

11. DISMANTLING

Day 4 of my journey to find me yesterday was not bad.
Found a few cockroaches close to Thanksgiving Day and
　　saw fault in someone smash smash.
Mind is somehow much calmer
MD Anderson infusion is over.
I see more words are popping out
　through your mouth like popcorn.

Maybe you are stabilizing
Maybe you are getting better
I am watching my mind
cautiously getting elated.
I am getting used to take
whatever comes to you

I am learning to summon
Happiness from my mind on demand
Feels good to just do my part
and let the world happen around me
Like the whole weight of the world on my shoulder is
　　removed, like a crane picked it up and dropped it on the
　　ground
What a profound wisdom I got this morning through
　　morning discussions.

There are three parts to me as I think of me. The physical
　　body is first, the psychological one has the mind, which
　　is the ego, and my real being, self, is third.

The psychological one with thoughts, feelings, and
　　identifications with each role, husband, wife, child
　　worker, boss, friend, teacher, doctor actor all form my

persona

This persona I am calling me. It is in mind. When I drop me, that persona drops. This sorrow, happiness, pain, misery drop.

Now I look at myself. That self is the real me

I never knew all my life; I lived with an imaginary person as me, the shadow of real me.

I noticed once when I saw my husband as a patient, and dropped the identification of my husband, my mental anguish got extinguished

So now the real practice is to just watch the moments of the ego in the form of me and mine, sorrow and elation.

The minute I remember that it is a projection of the mind, mind-made, not real, it dissolves.

Now I want to practice abiding in myself, not in the psychological person I created, the start of my dismantling!

12.   SINGING WITH A FRIEND

The speed of your words popping
from your mouth is increasing
simple sentences are forming
although your dysarthria is
preventing them from being fluent,
I see your efforts have quadrupled

You want to catch them from
your mind, arrange them & bring
them out through your mouth as
speech. The tongue & mouth yet
have to cooperate. You seem
happy. You talked with your

brother in India. You brought
the Marathi ABCD chart out to
practice with him so enthusiastically!
Your friends came CV & Danu
from Los Angeles so happy you were
with the newborn words. You

enjoyed cursing each other
Hugging & reminiscing the
old med school days.
You sang song for the
the first time not so well

but the words came out.
I saw that high energy
flowing through you like a dried plant

came alive after watering.
I see some improvement in you
Maybe the infusion is working well

My mental waves are subsiding
Not too high, not too low
I see things as they are
All this churning in my life
Has taught my mind
to calm down and just be.

The palliative care nurse helped
to paint the picture of hospice
We are sitting on the fence
One side is life, whichever way we want to live; the other side
    is hospice, accepting death as is
Sitting on the fence is our mind
Waiting! Today's upanishada lecture

Blew my mind away.
The body is a stack of 5 elements
created due to movement in consciousness
Through senses, we perceive in
our mind and body, you stop the sensory

Input to the mind, the mind and body fall off. What remains is
    you. The real you
Call it sat chit ananda or whatever
So, I am not so attached to your body
Nor to your mind
My impersonal awareness is growing
Let us smile through the tough times

Because we are happy.
Don't let body and mind obscure
this happiness. We can watch your body
heal or get sick.
Our happiness will not budge!

13. IMPERSONAL AWARENESS

Day 6 of my spiritual journey
All day yesterday, worldly
Friends visiting, Care Giving,
Singing, attending to guests
Awareness all outside
Did not have any mental anguish

Hardly any cockroaches of jealousy
Greed, desires, anger
But no awareness of self
Total identification with the body and
Mind all day. No impersonal awareness
Today Swami is telling how to get to that impersonal
    awareness

There is nobody as a thing.
It is a wave in consciousness
Like an incense stick glowing when lit
When you move it, it forms a circle
But there's no circle; you stop moving the incense stick, and
    the circle disappears. The senses sense the objects; the mind
    processes and forms an image or an idea. Thus, the body is
    an image in the mind. I wonder what scientific experiment
    can prove that. FMRI, EEG, PET, or an instrument yet to
    come?

Organs of action through the sense of touch
& all other senses, create an
action in mind where there isn't any

in sleep, the senses are
not there. The mind is asleep. There
is nobody, no world. Know

that body is an imagination
then the happiness you got
when you see ice-cream is due
to the external object giving pleasure
But go inwards beyond
the body & mind. You will

see a stage of pure joy
and contentment, but you
can only feel it after you
let go of external pleasures.
that mind needs to deoccupy
with external senses & occupy

internally on self.
Then you will Be &
that being opens up
the chit, The direct
knowledge, the bliss
thousand times more than

the external pleasure,
happiness on demand without
needing outside things.
How would that be?
Easy way to get it is
impersonal awareness

Be aware of body & mind
the thought the intellect.
the ego & know it is
an imagination in mind
that is it. Know who
you are. You are the

sat chit ananda.
Experience yourself
today I will focus on
the awareness of witnessing
everything that happens
to me. Good luck!

My personality the me
I think is a persona in
mind & is not me the
things I see are not me
& not mine. Just find the real me!

14.   DISSECTING MIND

Day 7 of my spiritual journey
Gratifying the first 3 hours of
my day in spiritual reading
with my sisters & then with
Upanishad group.
Tried impersonal awareness

yesterday. Happened 3 times
but needed the effort to remind
me. Most of the day
enjoyed working things with
friends. Gratifying to see
such good friends, so giving

but did get identified with it
Hiking to the top of the mountain
with Danu & being with nature
did bring me closer to the source.
Seeing Danu so happy brought joy
still felt I brought her joy

I can see the ego taking
the credit, enjoying happy
Missed watching the mind.
Today watching the mind meditation
of swami TV explained how to

see it as appearance; gave me
a tool.
mind is the memory of the past, a bag of

thoughts It brings to present, &
projects to the future bring in time
Nothing is new in mind.

You appear as a continuous
thing by connecting past memories
past, present & projecting in future.
That is how you know it is not
real.
Like a glow of incense stick

moving can write I love you.
Stop moving. There is no I love
you - The movie on the screen appears
real. but is multiple, still photos
together. stop the light and movie
stops. Thus, movement in

our mind makes it
appear like a continuity
In reality, everything is constantly
changing.
So, watch your mind.
thought, they are disconnected,

not yours. just watch those
ideas in mind. They are not
yours. emotions in mind, not yours.
Mind is fooling you as that
glow that these activities
are real. It is as it appears

Watching creates so much
power in you. That is freedom
So today, I will try to
watch my mind.
mind makes anxiety
due to attachment,

fear due to aversion
Just watch it. Don't condemn
anxiety & fear are minds.
Just watch objectively
& you will realize your
inner being your inner power
yourself!

15.   **CALMING DOWN**

You are so happy to see CV.
Danu and I hike to the top
of the mountain to stand in the hole
in the mountain, you & CV chat,
walk & watch us on top of the mountain
Danu and CV are impressed by the

unique mountain with holes in it
Papago Park is called, lake, picnic
next to the zoo, perfect weather.
We get famous chhole bature
from little India, we came back
in time to feed you. Reminds

me of our trips revolving around
Ashi's feeding time.
Then Rani's house. How you
try to talk. Now some
broken sentences. Everyone fills
in the blank or corrects in

their own mind interpreting as they feel.
They practice ABCD Indian
barakhadi with you, I see
shock & grief on their face
when they see you cannot read

ABCD. They encourage you.
We go for our walk
Listening to spiritual songs.

Your feeding time
I eat dinner. I go to sleep.
Simple, beautiful day. The mind
Vacillationstions have stopped.

Hansa's reading from book
of Jim Stovall helped
seeing joy in every situation
smiling during tough times
is a real asset.
I think we are getting there
Now the task is to console
others who are still grieving!

16.   I AM READY

Returned from MD Anderson.

You have improved some. Few words are coming out. MRI
is unchanged. The virus is undetected in the blood.

Maybe the disease has stopped. The rapid decline is halted.
Now the reality strikes. What am I left with? How much
deficit?

You still can't say your name or anyone's. you cannot say
my son or daughter or doctor or friend. Still pretty hard
to communicate.

Such opposite emotions are trying to mix like water and
oil. The elation, on the one hand, that you got your life
back as opposed to one month life that the doctor said.

But fear, on the other hand, will you not be able to speak
ever? Now intense speech therapy is the only way out.

I have all my energy vested in finding help. Good speech
therapist at Barrows, finding speech therapist in India
for tele for added practice

Bring in friends practice, practice, practice but also be
prepared to accept whatever the outcome. Even if you
can't talk, both of us are closer than ever.

Timely Upanishad reading today. You are not the doer.
The body Body-mind is doing it
You are not doing it

Nature is doing natural activities like trees growing
Children growing life happening.

Activities happen
Like teaching happens
I am not a teacher
If we do the actions 100%

Doership goes away
Can also do it by surrendering
To the higher power
Or knowing body mind or Prakriti is
doing it through this body

The attachment to the result goes away
The burden of responsibility goes away
The desires go away
The freedom in this difficult situation enters with a bang!

Fear is gone.

Thank you, swami TV, for these teachings today
I need not worry how I will deal with this new life, living
with your inability to talk, not knowing if you will ever
recover. Now I know my responsibility
I will give 100% in action to help you recover

It brings so much freedom and peace that I don't have to
be responsible for its success or not. Life will happen.

All this energy I am saving by not worrying goes now in

giving my 100% to him. Enjoying with you just the way you are every day.

The attachment to you being fully functional, and the desire for the reversal to your prior life is gone. I am watching the movie of my life, waiting for the next chapter to happen.

Wow! Just a little bit of this daily teaching beats any psychotherapy. The trick is to hold on to the teaching and act. And Act 100% is my motto from today.

The burden-ful life, the fear of disability, the fear of changing social status, fear of losing friends, and family are all replaced by embracing the new life, whatever it is.

Because all I have to do is give my 100% and then just watch. Thankfully enjoy playing the game of life. What a relief. I am ready for whatever comes my way!

17.   WHY DIFFERENT SETS OF RULES?

My mind is sitting on the fence, waiting for the treatment by the T cells to work or not on the JC virus that had decided to dominate your brain's speech area. So far, the virus has won, capturing the speech neurons and literally making you speechless. My thoughts are projecting a movie on the screen of my mind.

You, a one-time famous transplant surgeon from a renowned institution, became a recipient of a double lung transplant yourself. To protect the newly found lung from overzealous surveillance and attack from your own immune system, doctors summoned a powerful army of immuno-suppressor drugs.

Just like in life, when one wins in the game, the other loses. The viruses that live in your body, latent because of the immune system check, took the opportunity of the weakened immune system and activated the latent JC virus into a full-blown attack on your brain, causing Progressive Multifocal Leuko encephalopathy PML in short.

Such a rare is the disease that the pharmaceutical companies' lack of potential to make money prevented it from entering into the visibility spectrum of their potential candidates for developing the drugs. Left with the orphan disease, we looked for government-funded research for rare diseases.

The doctor with profound knowledge of PML at the National Institute of Health guided us to MD Anderson cancer center for an experimental trial. One donor gave you the lung. Now another donor is going to try to save your brain.

Donor T cells, the immune cells, will fight the JC virus and help your immune-suppressed T cells wake up and fight. What a delicate balance to maintain. Stimulate enough to fight the virus but not more as not to reject the well-received lung.

The first infusion of T cells made some headway in the fight against the virus. From no communication status, you started making simple communications. Enough to connect with our children and granddaughter! A special Thanksgiving it was. None of the drama, love flowing like a river, everyone wondering if it could be the last Thanksgiving with pops?

Charades, celebration of missed Diwali, everyone dressing up in colorful Indian costumes, girls looking like princesses with all the Jewelry, granddaughter learning about rangoli she called sand painting, she painted the whole family holding hands with each other, sparklers and lots of tea lights and of course the sweets ending with the famous family pictures.

Next day the Thanksgiving celebration, all dressed in western clothes dressed up to their best, everyone giving their speech of their thankfulness. You started the speech as usual. You started slow; you managed to make broken sentences. You did well. But you wanted to say more, wondering if this was your last speech.

The harder you were trying; the virus was making its presence evident. Those words were hesitating to come out. The first time, you broke down in front of children and cried. But you let them know by hugging gestures folding your hands in front of you, touching your heart, and giving a flying kiss to our granddaughter. Everyone was in tears but still joyful to know Pop loved them so much. Words could not have expressed that love any better.

We are on our way to MD Anderson for the second infusion on Sunday of Thanksgiving weekend. The busiest time to travel, but the need for rapid second infusion super-seeded the risk of covid.

We had to choose possible covid VS definite PML and death in a few months. We had traveled before for medical help and were comfortable as people wore masks at the airport.

We came to the airport, making our Uber driver wear a mask to protect ourselves. The driver apologized and wore it. He had half the lung removed for cancer at the same time you had your lung transplant. He was very collegial throughout the ride and even went out of his way to help us with our bags.

Being in first class and needing a wheelchair bypassed all the lines. So, we had two hours left before the flight. Worried about getting exposed to so many people for two hours, we decided to take the 59 $ per person day pass at the lounge, hoping to avoid crowds and buy some comfort.

Initially, we were happy we made the right decision. Slowly I started seeing more and more people with no masks, not masks around the neck but no masks. Rich people, some with families, children with masks around the neck not on the face or not, adults with no masks, young people traveling at the company's expense mostly not wearing masks, some older people and some young did wear masks.

Free food. People were eating and talking. Close to 9 am, the whole lounge was packed. No skipped seat between us. Mask less people in front, on the side, behind us. It appeared as if this was a licensed lounge to be without masks.

No one enforced the mandate to wear a mask at the lounge. The staff was bending backward to please the rich people who were paying the airline enough to pay their salaries. No one wanted to ruffle the feather by asking these people to wear masks.

We wondered if it would have been better to be with more masked people in masses downstairs near the gate than in the lounge. I am getting the news on my I watch about the new strain of Covid very virulent, defying the vaccine. Israel closed their borders. Many countries are thinking about it.

It was time for us to leave at 9. The lady wheeled you downstairs. We saw a big crowd, but they were all masked. We did get physical comfort, but after fighting lung transplant and PML, getting Covid because some privileged feel law doesn't apply to them would be devastating! For your severely immunosuppressed body, Covid equals a death sentence.

We keep our fingers crossed that you beat the PML and don't get covid. I did let the American airline staff at the counter know. She said she is so overwhelmed, and there is no supervisor. I am sure it was hard for her to confront so many maskless people who thought they had a right to break the law because they were paying plenty. I was sure I would buy the membership next time, just waiting for the airline miles to rise.

We would have to make these trips every three weeks, but my experience forced me to change my mind. If this happened in one lounge, I am sure it must also be happening in other places. Writing about it is my way of increasing awareness. Meanwhile, we pray that you get better with this new treatment at MD Anderson and remain Covid free.

18.   KNOWLEDGE IS ONLY IN THE PRESENT

Today's teaching reminds me to
live in the present and create a
space between me and the body.
You identify with the body
through its attributes.

The body is old, but you say
I am old.
You put attributes to the body
beautiful, then you say
I am beautiful.

Look at the multiple
identifications & work
through them.
Verbal statements will not do.

Make a list of how many days
I identified with the body
or its attribute.
I should witness it.

I identify with color
of body, age & gender
make a list & dismiss all
Then see what happens.

The body will remain in good health

Gracefully you will accept
problems of the body and
you will not become a burden to
others or yourself.

The albatross around your
neck will go. & you
will become free.
Albatross, is identifications
with the body.

A fruit in your hand,
there is nothing to conceive
or imagine. It is there
You know it.

You should be able to say
I don't know. Only then
will your mind opens.
Don't make Vedanta conceptual

Make a log, what are
all the values & systems
in which I identify with
the body & start dismantling
all of them.

I like this, don't like it
that means I am identifying
with it. It should not

disturb your inner comfort

Develop a nack for it.
Develop a nack of dealing
with object or event.
Replace illness of the body
with it.

Don't you ever
make a deal with birth
& death.
There is nothing like
birth & death. The
body dies; I do not die.

If I am this ball of
flesh & blood, then
I am nonself. The
body is the false self.

Understand this deep
within.
You have to test your
understanding.
You have to try this.

This is vedanta

Is there a space within
you and the body?
People want space, then

they go outside to explore
space.

How much space do you
have? Inner space?
You get frustrated so easily
It shows you have no inner space
you have to develop
that space.

The body becomes ill. Ok.
Body is ill. Create that inner space.
Stay with body is ill.If you conclude,
I am ill there is no space.
You shall create the space.
I am the one always aware of the
body. Here is the body.

Create that cognitive space.
Do you know what that space is?
That space is equivalent to freedom.
You don't need the outer space
as much as you imagine.

You need a little inner space
To begin with. Do this much
challenge. Create this inner
space. Work on it. This is
the so-called spiritual

Practice. How? Be a
witness to the body
& witness to the changes
that are happening in the
body.

The body is ever changeful
It is like a wave
Some of the changes are
uncomfortable. That is illness

That is Ok. Treat the illness.
Don't battle the illness.
You battle the illness.
You don't have space.
Treat the illness and you
created a space.

That is the same as the fruit in
hand. See it directly, not conceptualize.
Realize.
Be a witness to all the

changes that are happening
in your body.
Now I see how I was
battling the illness of Dilip
I had no space.

Treat the illness we

are doing it. All the
other thoughts, imagination
about the future, worries

are all identifications
with the body. The
illness is a stage in
the body. I witness it.

Knowledge is always
in the present, never
in the future.
Examine your knowledge.
Experience it.

You only know in the present
now. There is no knowledge
in the future. There is no future
, so don't put off self-knowledge

in the future as a goal.
Self-knowledge is now
in the present so get on
with it.

19. BE A WITNESS TO YOUR MIND

Today's lecture by swami TV gives me a tool for controlling
  my desires.

Be witness to the mind
sometimes up, sometimes down
sometime in between.
Be witness to that &
go within.

Once you discover yourself,
then only you know the meaning of aham
What you are not is the discovery.
Everything you perceive & conceive is nonself.

Identification of body, mind, through
ideas, leave it. Keep doing until
you need not tell that I am
Sachidananda. I am not a woman,

mother, Indian, American. How long do I tell
that to myself? Until you feel
you are not that. until you
don't identify with my name, my age

or space, from where I am
what is there in the name,
I have to tell myself.
I am not the name.

I am sat chit ananda
you need to go within
when someone calls me by my name
I have to remember, oh, he is calling me.

You have to do it.
There is no other way
Witness. your essential nature
contemplate that I am the

witness to the ever-charging mind.
Mind brings time. Psychological time.
So, drop the mind, and time drops.
Desirelessness drops time.

When do you desire? Only when
you think we are limited.
So, die to all desires now.
You will become Amrutam deathless

Desire is in the future.
Fear is a projection in the future
of the past
So desireless & fearless, you
are not identified with time.

So die to yesterday &
many thousands of tomorrows
& many thousands of yesterdays
die & die & die so you come alive

That is crucifixion. Unless
there is crucifixion, how
can there be a resurrection?
A mere verbal statement

will not do. You have to
discover that.
As long as there is a body, sense of
identity with the body is there.

Rise to the occasion.
Here is the body. You call it body.
What is the body?

The mask is made of cloth. Strings are
made of cloth. We put it
over our mouths. We give a name mask.
It is merely a piece of cloth.

You give a unique name to it.
Is it intrinsically a mask
or a piece of cloth with a name to it.

Now what is body? It is a conglomerate.
A stackof 5 elements. Up to loin is
earth, abdomen water, stomach

fire of hunger; container of fire.
Chest is not just bones & flesh,
pulmonary or respiratory,

is called vayu. Wind container for wind

Mouth, nostrils, sinuses, space
The body is a stack of earth, water, fire
& wind. You are not the body
There is a sense of identity. Leave it.

It is not difficult nor easy.
It is just a fact.
In work, in the temple every
one will say it is a body.

Only in Vakyavruti will it say you
are not the body.
What do I get out of it?
You get great freedom, relief

You look at life.
You live beyond the threshold of
body consciousness most of the time.
Like soccer player is not body conscious,

but goal conscious while he is playing.
Even if he is injured, he goes after the
goal. Like a soldier, is not body conscious
but is winning conscious

while working, we are beyond body identification.
Whatever is left, those times, dis-identify. Isn't it simple?
You are not supposed to have body consciousness.
Nonidentification with body doesn't hurt the body.

Be generous to your body but don't identify with it,
clothe it feed it, treat it, caress it & leave it.
Don't identify with it.
Identification makes the body an albatross

Knowledge of self is all you are not
Can you control what happens to your body?
But one thing you can do is
you can stop identifying with the body
you can.

Once you stop identifying with your body,
the feeling of lightness emerges,
normally people are a bundle of cravings & fear

By stopping to identify with the body
the albatross of craving (desire) & fear
is removed, leaving you with lightness.

We live with a mixture of
Craving & fear because
you identify with the body
so it would help if you stopped identifying

Soccer player, businessman
soldier can do it, so you can do it.
So you become free from
albatross of fear & craving.

The fear of death goes away

I am the body is the idea
not yours, social life & relative life
does not help.

Half-filled pot with water
is the same as the body, half filled with water
So far, very little time has been occupied
by myself, most by nonself
Keep trying. Don't give up.

20.   SCHOOL OF LIFE

Are we lucky or not?

Ashwini brought this yoga guru from India.

To give you personal yoga and quantum healing. His emphasis is on how the mind can treat or cause any illness and teaching us to quieten and strengthen the mind

He is taking us to a higher level of awareness.

How gently he is increasing the physical level of yoga, and I notice both of us have improved posture and already are losing our complaints of pain and aches. His demonstration of standing on toes, on finger on the head at the age of 72 is

a proof of how powerful our mind is. We need to believe how strong our mind is. When doubts creep us, it gets weak and takes us down to limited consciousness. He is also doing quantum healing on you. I am reading Deepak Chopra's book on quantum healing.

We already have a test subject you in our laboratory. We are worried your PML is not getting under control. That virus is refusing to leave you. But with a quiet and robust mind, and accessing awareness you can kill that virus with

the quantum energy. Let us both help each other stay in that higher level of consciousness. Today's meditation was space meditation. Space is the subtlest element of the five elements the body is made of, and that connects us with the big one mind or higher awareness.

Sit upright, close your eyes, and feel the space around you. You don't need to think you know the space around you, in the sky, all over. That space is you, the knowingness, the atma chaitanya, whatever you want to call it.

Thoughts can only perceive. But space doesn't need perception to receive knowledge. You directly know. Your body and all things are in this space, superimposed. So, the reality is you are this vast space, knowingness.

Tap into it. Why would you stay in the limited consciousness? Everything you want to know, do, and want is accessible through this vast awareness. So where is the place for doubts, worries, and sickness?

It feels like studying back in med school, just the subject is changed to the mental and spiritual science of life instead of the physical science of life. Every day we learn something new. But we will have to work as hard as med school in this school of life and enjoy just as much as we did then and succeed at the top of the class just like then.

21.   EXPERIMENT LIFE

The Quantum healing book deepens my belief about how powerful our minds can be. Our body heals naturally like a bone heals after a fracture, but we don't call it a miracle. Same way, when the cancer is cured against the medical definition, we

Call it a miracle. The only difference is the latter involves the mind. Very few can do it unless they have a strong longing to live or have a significant amount of positivity. You belong to that class. You love to live, and you don't have a single bone of negativity.

I need to work hard to catch up with your positivity, but now I have an incentive. Because without it, it will be hard to get ahead. Morning reading was about how to shed the anxiety, fear, and negativity, which happens once you increase your awareness that it is

happening in the mind, and you are only the witness. As the awareness, as a witness, increases, the negativity of the mind proportionately decreases. If it is that simple, let me start today. I will track my mind and thoughts. Let us see how long it takes.

The second way I learned to not identify with the mind is to know that mind and body are a complex and the mind takes care of the body. The story of a lizard egg falling in the sink pipe, coming out as a baby immediately catching two flies in the sink, shows nature takes care of you.

You plan in the present moment, and the mind will help you. Then totally let go. Just do what you planned

100%, and trust you will be taken care of. The mind will take care of the body. You are free, just a witness of the body, mind, and all the activities.

This freedom will loosen the grip of fear, anxiety, worry, and suffering. Loss of this negativity will start getting you in silence, and after that, the joy and feeling of contentment occur. Slowly the mind will be under your control so will the body.

It is hard to believe, but we didn't believe everything in med school, still accepted it, and studied. So instead of being skeptical, let us give our 100% and then either prove it is right or wrong. Let's do the experiment like our chemistry lab!

22.   BE UNCONSCIOUS TO THE MIND

I get joy in typing today's date 2/22/22

Today we are going to join the walking group. I know you are very uncomfortable because men walk together, and you will be separated from me. There will be no one to complete your sentences

enhancing and exposing your disability of speaking. My mind is on a different track. I might be seen as an outcast since I am spiritual, and there is not much in common with them. I am analyzing my discomfort in the mind; why? The ego

does not want to be hurt. Then I am saying it is happening to the mind and not me. I am witnessing it. But the thought, anxiety, and sensation have not gone away. It is lessened though. Does this witnessing really work?

I think it is more of my aversion to becoming nobody or aversion to discomfort in my mind. Is the discomfort in mind my discomfort? Today's reading says to be unconscious of what is going on in mind, like you are unconscious of pancreatic enzymes digesting your food

So, the mind does its own job. It goes into a future that doesn't exist but adds time and thus sorrow, so knowing this, if I still feel discomfort, it is because I am identifying with the mind. Now bring this mind inwards, and just watch it doing silly

things and just ignore it; you can do it. This is working

somewhat. If life is happening, I am not the doer, then let the mind do what it wants to. You have nothing to do with it. You be in your own nature, joy, and peace; tap into it and stay there.

I have the power to control everything. Nothing can touch me or injure me. Then why this emotion? Emotions and thoughts keep occurring, but as you practice ignoring them, know who you are, just the witness, and let the mind do its digestion.

The peace will come. Being comfortable with uncomfortable thoughts or emotions is key. You are not them. So instead of manipulating them, just ignore them, let them do their job, and you continue to do yours. These uncomfortable situations are

giving me opportunities to strengthen my mind and realize my inner self. I was not conscious of my mind and thoughts and let the anxiety take over that eventually affects my health. Now first, I am conscious of them, feel the discomfort, learn to witness, dis-identify with the mind,

ignore and be unconscious of it. Just the difference is instead of anxiety, I feel powerful joyful that the outside things, including my mind, cannot take away my joy. Is this real or just mental? I will see how long this peace and joy last or the mind bothers me again? More tomorrow.

23.   **WALK IN THE PARK**

We went to dessert ridge park, met eight people. You walked with men, I with women. You had no problem. I enjoyed talking about dogs and birds. Now whatever the acrobats mind did about the walk yesterday was self-imposed torture in hindsight. People do that all the time.

How unaware we are of our mind. The mind can take you to heaven and hell in one day. Being enslaved by such an entity sounds so ridiculous. Granted, this was the first time we learned this. But now we know. I feel so stupid to get into the spell of mind and agreed with the mind that I would not have a good time, as true.

Now I see the importance of swami TV's words. Ignore that mind. I think following that mind is like behaving like a child while being an adult. That is how we live our life. The mind is like the child. Being a witness and ignoring it gets you out of trouble. Let the prakruti run the life.

Let us be like the hummingbirds sucking the nectar of joy and peace from our own reservoir effortlessly and enjoy watching the movie of life from our safe, comfortable inner palace. You did well better than me. Your aphasia didn't bother you.

Your walking alone with them gave us overconfidence. Not realizing you can't walk so well, you kept walking without holding my hand on the way to the parking lot, tripped, missed the sidewalk step, and fell on your hands and chest

Bleeding from both hands, mask and phone scattered all over, panting, looking so scared I held your head on my lap reassuring you. A car passed by, willing to help, saying he was a nurse. I had no chance to assess you if you broke anything. You slowly got up, stood on your

Own and walked to the car. We came home I cleaned and dressed your wounds your hands are all wrapped in gauze bandage like a mummy. I thought I handled it well. Other than the guilt I felt for not holding your hand, I acted like a doctor, focused on treating you shutting the mind. That lack of identification with

the mind, gave me power due to no mental movement. I am experiencing when I am focused on one thing; the mind stays under your control. How quickly you recovered from the mental movements amazed me. You did so well at speech therapy. Found out singing from the intact right side of brain

Magically brings out words. We were happy to get this new tool. The yoga teacher did relaxation and told you to write down 10 things to make you happy. Shelby helped us change bulbs with the long stick with bulb-changer at the end.

On the whole, there were short times we were in our bigger self, most of the time in the smaller self, but mind movement was less. There is no fear even if you fell. Quantum physics book says how you can visualize your healing and mind can heal

the body. So that is your experiment and see how quickly

you feel well. Mind is to not get identified with any negative thoughts if they arise.

24.   SWARM OF DUCKS.

Call from MD Anderson, Niki's cells are ready. They passed the criteria of their patented algorithm. We are going on 3rd coming back on 10th of March. Last night my mind was like a storm, questioning where to stay, hotel or Airbnb, digging out

The painful memories of bad experience with Airbnb, spring break, can't get flights, crowded airports, omicron still there, renting a car, leaving you alone to pick up the car, intruding in my normal sleep. But this morning after my 3 hours of bathing

in spiritual talks, that storm is totally subsided and the calm of the lake I am watching from our windows is invaded by a large flock of flying ducks landing on the water simultaneously making the lake look like sea spitting the white froth.

I have never seen so many ducks together at the same time, effortlessly flowing like ballerinas, the nature's show intensified by the entrance of more than a dozen large white birds may be cranes, all sitting at the edge all around our little lake as if they

are the teachers teaching the little ducks in the water now parked intently watching these big white birds? The show ends with all birds flying away at the same time, again making large waves in the lake with white froth while flapping their wings.

They were simultaneously making an audible symphony with their wings and their vocal cords. What a nature's show!

Yesterday we wrote down 10 things that make us happy, most were spirituality, our family members, nature, special people in our lives and the thought is rushing through my head, where was the focus all of our lives? Career, success, name and fame, parties, trips and cruises, large houses, expensive cars. None of them were in our list. Wish we had made this list when we

were young. Our life's car was on the wrong highway. Not sure if our list would have been different then. So busy we were chasing the ghosts we had no time to examine our life as if we were in a boat of life where the captain was society, and we went where it took us.

Letting my mind do its own thing, and I am taking charge, feels good. But today's lessons are even better. Seeking joy outside and getting it results in 1-now wanting something else even better2-law of diminutive returns3-it becomes

monotonous. As opposed to going inwards and abiding in your nature the true joy- there is nothing more superior, one without the other, not needing anything, I have everything, all is mine, all are part of me, no question of taking birth again and abiding in your superior abode.

Coming from another saint book about the experiences of many enlightened masters, if in your heart, if you fully believe I am the one in many forms, many people at many places, your accumulated karmas and desires burn right away. Make sure every day, you have control over your senses. Ignore mind and intellect, and go in silence. Only there the direct experience occurs. Talk less, read spiritual in the morning and evening, meditate, do satsang and rest of the time, go in silence, and contemplate.

Gather your blisses that is your happiness. But what I liked about sadguru was the way out of sorrow in the outward world is to go inwards. The experience whichever always happens within with or without outside activity, and you have

control over what experience you want to have. What a power! If we can practice these principles, we can heal our bodies, we can remain happy, and outside things should not bother us. So, I will plan the trip without the mind turbulence. Even though

Outsiders say poor you; I don't feel that way. Throughout these tough times, I see us evolving and creating, or I should say enjoying the joy we are. The pleasures we are getting in little things is making the traditional pleasures unnecessary.

25.   GOOD MORNING AMERICA

Sitting on the sofa, watching through the glass wall, I see the greenish blue water in the lake, still calm enough to see the reflections clear enough to recognize the house and Palm and olive trees but stirred enough by the ducks to produce tiny gentle waves.

The gentle wind blowing on the water feels like someone is rolling a thin transparent silk cloth creating small folds in the fabric. Everyone is trying to assert their presence in the water, transforming the water into a multicolor art piece.

The sun rays occupying a small area transform it into golden shimmering waves as if trying to wipe off the tree's reflection, but making sure its own reflection remains. All different trees have cast their reflection into all values of green, light green, lemon green, deep green, olive green, sap green, pthalo green. Blues of the sky, tan of houses, dark greys and browns of rocks, and different shades of yellow by the sun.

But better than a painting in the water, I see the wind making its marks by changing the directions of the waves at its own whim. The movement of the water is mostly the creation of so many ducks. Landing, they make a splash with a white frothy fountain, gliding fast they create an ever-growing V, or just sitting and trading,

creating circles pushing outwards. when all the ducks take off at the same time, they make collective large white waves trying to go as high as they can. Flying in the air, they, make a beautiful symphony with their flapping wings and chirping mouths.

By now, the sun has finalized its domination. Now the whole lake is shimmering gold film extending the sunshine on the grass all around the lake except for the shadows of the trees where trees guard their space even against the mighty sun.

Nine turtles crawled up from the lake over the one-foot stone edge, always at the same place next to the large tree protecting its space. The contrast of the shadow and the bright sun may be attracting the space to these turtles, as the sunshine appears brighter than it is.

Each turtle climbed up one after the other, sitting on the grass at the edge of the lake, all sitting in a perfectly straight row as if they had an electronic ruler in their brain. Sunbathing begins, they have closed their eyes, and now they are in bliss. They will be there until 3 pm, and one after another, they will crawl back into the water.

The whole flock of ducks had their bath, and play; now time to nap. They all choose to gather under the tree in the shadow, right next to the turtles. There are no quarrels or disputes; both turtles and ducks live in harmony right next to each other. Ducks flop on the ground, retract their limbs and, turn into round blobs, close their eyes. Meditation starts—no more noise.

No vacation could surpass this experience. I love when these ducks face and look at me, just sitting there. They make me forget all my pain and take me to a higher level of my consciousness. This is my God Morning America show!

26. HOW TO CONTROL THE MIND

Swami TV talk today was the best of all I have heard, but he always comes up with something new, never making me feel I know it all. The mind is like a computer. It gets input from the 5 senses. In the mind, it modifies the sensations, compares them

from past experiences, labels them as pain or pleasure experience, and out comes the output as a thought; this is good or bad. Mind is nothing but the memory of past sensations and experiences. So, it is always judging, blaming, criticizing, appreciating, craving, and creating all sorts of emotions.

The mind creates thoughts. Thought creates time. Thought always comes from memory in the mind. So, it will always come from the known. You cannot have creativity coming out of your mind. It will be limited.

If you watch your mind and see where one thought leads to another, jumping from one to another, you will see the movement of the mind.

Movement of mind creates time and you cannot have your own creative power. If the mind calms down to only one thought and that keeps going without jumping; you have access to your inner creative power, unlimited. How to access it? It can happen in meditation. There is a conversation to have between the higher power, I, atma whatever you call it but that is what you are talking to the mind.

You are dead without my power. So, who are you to tell me and guide me, conflicting me? Be quiet. Do as I say.

The mind slows down in thoughts. But it becomes very alert. Now you guide it to where you want it to be. Now you are the master of the mind and not the slave.

When the mind is quiet, in that silence, you are in the heart, and the creativity flows. So, your life should be a meditation. That means just be. Not thinking but observing your mind thus slowing it down and let the knowledge flow through you! Enjoy that joy that you are!

27. LADY, YOU ARE ON YOUR OWN!

Just finished listening to swami TV's talk. Today's teaching has taken me to a depth of silence, a feeling of deep joy and peace, and I hope it doesn't go away. Nothing nothing is bothering me. So much inner calmness, I could live in it for ages without

needing anything from outside. It is the feeling I used to get after meditation which didn't last long. I have no desires, as if I have everything far superior to any outside luxury can give me. But how do you integrate into worldly life and

still get to hold on to this feeling. He says as long as you constantly watch your mind and feelings and do not judge or condemn your mind, you can be in this world and be in this state of meditation.

Society wants you to compare, condemn, and judge, always wanting more. Mind's nature is to create thoughts and feelings. These create psychological time. In the future, I will attain this, or in the past, it happened. The psychological time which, in reality,

doesn't exist, throws you out of kilter, and creates unhappiness and desires. Desire creates fear. So, living in this world while enjoying everything if I stay a witness to my mind, meaning thoughts and feelings, just watching, not even correcting them

he says we could remain in this silence. Naturally, doubts are arising in my mind about how it can be possible and I am watching that thought too. Let us see how long this feeling will last. We are in Houston for your last infusion. This infusion is from our son Niki's cells. I am not sure you need one more. She feels Niki came all the way here from Pittsburgh to donate his blood for you.

His cells are grown and ready to fight the virus in you. So, she wants to give you this one as the last infusion. His cells will have a half match with you. But half will be foreign to you as they are from me. I hope your body does not reject my genes strongly. Physically, emotionally we get along so well. Now I wonder how yours and my genes in your body will cohabitate!

This hope I am watching in my mind can create psychological time and take away happiness. I am witnessing it. You are doing better and better in every way, like a chick coming out of an egg and learning and enjoying a new life.

You are getting mentally so sharp, you have become my calendar, reminding me of things I shouldn't forget in spite of your broken words. You are making sentences but the nouns and pronouns are replaced by this and that. Then I have to guess

what that this and that is. And during that game of our life's communication, so many unrelated objects and sentences come up, that make us laugh like crazy. It is like Saturday night live every day in our life, I wish I could write them down I would

have a great comedy. Comedy is unexpected response which is what both of us are creating, natural comedy creation! Like you have to say a word from each letter and you said fuck for F after a long searching. Then you have to

make a sentence with the word you create, which is hard
for you. You start with whatever comes to your mind.
You started saying old lady not remembering what the
word was. When I told you it was fuck, you had a task of
creating a sentence about old lady and fuck and we both
couldn't stop laughing.

In Houston the rodeo is going on after two years. Traffic
is at its highest it can be. We are in the car, me driving
on the new highways near downtown Houston trying
to follow newGPS in the rental car making me change
lanes 3 to the right two to left in this traffic, dizzying
me, looking at you for help.

you are feeling helpless. But we use one and a half hour
coming back from the hospital practicing your words
and sentences fromeach letter cracking jokes through
your new strange sentences, making you forget your
pain of the spinal tap and my anxiety of driving in
Houston at the peak traffic time with the rodeo going
on. We are at Viren and Danielle's house what a relief!

We made it all the way to Woodlands but spent 45
minutes figuring out how to go to Panda Express where
you insisted on eating as you liked the lunch earlier
the same day. Your insistence on finding it and my
expectations of you giving it up

and eat anything we find brought the mood of Saturday
night live to a horror movie. Finally, we find it, and
you eat the same thing you got for lunch, honey-
coated fried shrimp with fried rice. I watched you truly
enjoying eating honey coated shrimp in the car

and that made me feel going through all the frustrations was worth it. That satisfaction on your face was worth taking a picture in my mental camera and storing. It also has given me an impetus to learn more about handling a phone while

driving as you are absent from helping me anymore. I say to myself, Lady you are on your own! Better get proficient!

28. STRONG ME!

3/9/22

Our one-hour drive to MD Anderson has become a date for us, like the 4 limited bus ride when we started dating. Yesterday's tough ride in Houston traffic was a breeze. I am getting used to the possibility of missing an exit, and getting lost but I have become

confident I eventually am brought on track and have always made it back home. So now my mind is not jumping like a monkey looking for certainty but is enjoying the ride. We have resumed singing the four songs we learned from

our singing teacher before we stopped singing due to the arrival of the uninvited guest virus. We have been laughing so much due to your false starts in making sentences. Speech therapy is happening in one hour ride like the medical school study on the bus.

I watched YouTube and figured out how to deal with GPS problem that annoyed us the day before. I am proud of what I am becoming, a strong woman pushing through the obstacles, resolving the difficult issues saying Lady you are on your own!

Few points to practice today from my morning talk. Know that the mind will never be quiet and peaceful. Instead of compelling the mind to quieten, know you are peace and learn to bring the mind in you to access the peace.

As the mind is turned inwards, day by day, it will not go outwards for joy but will turn inwards to feel peace. So,

I feel we are lucky that now we have so few things we have to worry about outwardly life, and we can enjoy the inner peace.

So let us continue our journey together inwards and let go of the outward crutches like money, people, name fame, and trips to make us happy. It is so satisfying to see how little things can make people happy. I hope people get that without going through what we went through!

29.   **INFUSION**

3/11/22

You received your last infusion of our son's cells. I was watching the small plastic bag filled with clear liquid hung on the pole, dropping one drop at a time into your vein, drip, drip. Just in 15 minutes, the bag was empty.

It was a strange feeling. It reminded me of Prayag where three rivers meet making it a rare and auspicious place. So were you I and Niki meeting in your vein. Niki's cells carried half of yours and half of my genes and information.

Now we will see how well our genes get along. I hope there is no fight to prove one-upmanship. If we get along so well physically and mentally, does that mean our genes will too? In one week, we shall know if they cohabitate or are at war.

Yesterday you asked me to check if the three-digit additions you were doing were right. How hard you are working to regain what you have lost. I noticed for the first time you couldn't do 7+4=11. I taught you how to calculate using your fingers, and you had no

clue how to calculate using fingers. I felt so sorry for you. I said I would buy you abacus with beads to teach you additions. Sometimes I feel it is such a big task ahead of you. It takes years for children to learn. I had to cry alone.

But I remembered I promised I would not feel sorry for

you and also remembered that the body has to obey and react to the thoughts the brain sends. I quickly wiped my tears and decided to send the right thoughts to the body. You are healthy.

And all your speech and knowledge is expressing slowly some more every day. But I also told you, spiritually speaking, for your enlightenment, additions with numbers are not needed. Let us focus on our spiritual practices, and we started meditating.

30.   SEND THE RIGHT THOUGHT TO YOUR BODY!

3/12/22

My hopes of a big celebration and a picnic with our friends were crushed when Dr. Olson said there is some T2 activity in pons, in your brain stem on your MRI. It could be an artifact, but when she heard your new symptoms of diplopia localized in pons,

her eyes widened, her lips turned from C to inverted C, she was looking to the left and upwards, lost in her thoughts and changed her planned victory speech to a speech of conceding. This worries me, she said. She had come prepared to celebrate.

Reading the card, I gave her about how she saved Dilip's life made her cry. She opened the present of small crystal candle holders with hesitation. Before that, she had said she was not sure you would get better as you were not responding.

We decided to watch you clinically and repeat MRI in three weeks, then decide if you need one more infusion. She would like to do the MRI in Houston. One more trip. The federal mask mandate was still on when we returned, happy I was that it was our last flight and people wore masks. Omicron is not all gone. People have stopped wearing masks. I don't know if they will be wearing masks in the plane during the next trip. You are most at risk now being with maskless people.

Maybe we will drive—17 hour ride. Let us cross that bridge, then. Right now, let us send the right thoughts to our bodies. We are happy; we are healthy, we are having fun!

Your thoughts are more powerful to heal your body than anything else, so let's crank them up!!!

31.   TRUE GRIT

3/16/22

Boy, did you surprise me yesterday! One day you didn't know how to count, I was looking for an abacus for you, and the next day you could make five-digit additions. Could Niki's cells have pushed out the virus from your brain, and your brain cleared up enough to add?

Our 45 min Tesla ride to speech therapy, like our 4 ltd bus ride in India during med school, gives us the opportunity to connect without distractions. I call it a joy ride. How we look forward to these rides. In the car, you told me that the challenge of learning to talk, energizes you. You want to succeed, and you will go all the way to get to your goal.

You don't waste a minute. You don't want me to plan social activities as if you are studying for an exam. And I am sure, in spite of the virus eroding your speech neurons from your brain, you are determined to form a whole new track in your brain. I haven't known many people with grit like yours. Your drive to overcome challenges fires up joy cells in your brain.

That is why, at the start of your career, you chose to do transplant surgery instead of plastic surgery. You are known for your grit, why you don't give up in any difficult surgery and why other surgeons called you to rescue them when they were at the point of giving up.

How many families thanked you for saving their lives when no one else wanted to do such complicated surgeries. When you retired, your message to your residents was to develop Grit to be a successful surgeon. You even gave them each a book, true grit.

Now I feel like I am getting a private tutoring from you on grit, which I need badly. Fleeting from one project to the other as it gets tough has become a habit for me. But watching you deal with your health challenges with grit, I am getting used to going through the challenges without letting fear capture me.

But yesterday, you also surprised me by asking me which are the fingers. You thought toes were your fingers. You didn't know which is your tongue and even ears. We hadn't practiced body parts for a while. Those new tracks in your brain are like saplings. They need nurturing so let's not forget to name all the body parts daily.

What a dichotomy! On the one hand you are so sharp, teaching me so much; on the other hand, you don't know your body parts! I feel like I have a little genius kid in the big body. Your slip-ups in trying to come up with the words are cracking us up enough to keep us sane. Like you were supposed to say I baked a bun, and you kept saying butt!

Even this young pretty speech therapist could not stop laughing. You are a perfect example of what a response to life is as opposed to a reaction. Sadguru's book Taru is reading said if you have the willingness to respond to situations than react, it gives birth to infinite possibilities.

We listened to Tigerwood's speech yesterday about how for him, nothing was impossible, and I looked at you and said you are like him. Now I understand every adversity is for learning and growing if you choose to, called a response. Or you could choose to run away, get depressed, don't try anything hard, and react to life.

You always used the challenge to respond and grow. And you have inspired me to use the challenge to grow and feel comfortable with the uncomfortable feeling of challenge. You have become my cliff notes for life, along with all the other gurus. Sri Sri told us how to get rid of fear.

He said first, know you are much bigger than the body and mind and have all the power to deal with any challenge.

If that is not enough, know that you are always taken care of by nature, God, master, universe, atma, or soul. Choose the word that fits you. If you still have fear, work on the solution and watch the emotion by watching the sensation the fear creates. The fear dissipates.

Have an attitude that I am going to use the challenge to grow irrespective of the outcome. Sometimes you win sometimes you lose. You will get stronger, and fear will not obstruct you.

If still have fear, know that how people look at my failure has nothing to do with me. It is their problem. Their approval does not dictate who I am. So do not try to protect the image by suffering. Know you are strong on your own.

Still have fear, tell your mind thanks for warning me. But no thanks. I am in charge. I will take it over from here.

You relax. By now, the fear should go away. Without fear, your consciousness rises, and you can tap into many possibilities.

So, I like to deal with my challenges now and don't feel sorry for myself. 'Go through' is my motto now. You are my guru, baby! I love you so much.

32.   GROWING WITH THE TREE

3/16/22

I am greeted by a blooming tree outside of my window when I open my eyes from my afternoon little nap. Looking out through the large glass window, almost spanning the whole wall, I see the delicate spring leaves almost touching the glass as if trying to kiss me.

The fat round tree trunk with the weathered brown scales splits into two slightly narrower branches as if having two children on a family tree. Forming a perfect V, the two branches allow the sky to pass through to meet me.

The two main branches further split into twos and threes, further narrowed branches forming a network of branches like my mother and father from two to twenty-two. So far, I had seen dense green tree hiding more than fifty birds, not

allowing even the sky to shine through. Then I saw those proud, lively leaves almost feeling immortal and mighty, slowly losing their power, turning brown and wrinkly, and almost in two days all lost their grip on life. The storm helped them

detach from life easily. The bald tree with almost no leaves, exposing its skeleton, except for a few old wrinkled leaves hung in there like few people over one hundred years old holding on to life. I was getting used to meeting the sky through

The barren tree from my bed, and all of a sudden, yesterday all of a sudden, all the branches out of nowhere, had the tiny delicate Lemmon yellow leaves as if the mothers delivered so many babies. The ducks kept their Loyalty sitting in the small remaining shadow of the trunk.

I can see each and every tirtiary and quarternary little final delicate branch projecting downwards, almost like a willow tree, but stopping short at the bifurcation of the main trunk as if grandparents were watching, not allowing them to go any further.

Even the gentlest of the wind is enough to give these delicate tiny leaves a push to swing back and forth as if Mother Nature is rocking these babies. The tiny little leaflets are enjoying the sun and the fresh air aimlessly swinging in the air.

Today, in one day, all the leaves must have grown at least half an inch, adding a small tinge of green to their lemon yellow color. But just like kids, some are larger, and some are still in infancy, barely budding. They are all making their way to life ahead.

I feel like they are breathing with me. Half of my breath, my exhalation, the CO_2 becomes their inhalation. And I inhale their oxygen, exhaled by them, as if we are connected. As if this tree at the edge of this lake shares nature with ducks, turtles and

other trees standing right outside my window, sharing part of my life, giving joy to me, playing with me, and I bet it must feel my love every day when I greet it and grow with it.

33.   BUCKLE UP FOR THE FLIGHT OF NEW LIFE!

3/19/22

Today I understood what direct perception means. All these saints keep talking world is not real, body, and mind not real, used to provoke a revolt in me. You want me to believe that? That is blind faith. Swami TV was so clear, honest and blunt in explaining reality.

Body, mind, and energy all three layers are physical. Beyond which is consciousness. Reflection of consciousness in the mind and movement of the mind in consciousness creates the perception of the world. It is only a thought consciousness, material consciousness, friend consciousness, and enemy consciousness.

Consciousness is divided into many different parts and is labeled by mind as a tree, bird, man good, bad, etc. If you quieten the movement of mind, the perception through senses and interpretation through the mind stops. Direct perception starts.

You hear a sound that does not get labeled. You get joy through that sound. You become that sound; you go over the hills with that sound. That is direct perception. You can practice with all other four perceptions by telling the mind to Shut up. Once the mind is still, direct perception is possible. It is like a movie on a screen.

Because of the light, the movie is seen. If you stop the movie, take away the movie from the projector; light does not stop shining on the screen.

The mind is playing a movie through the quality of giving nama Rupa, name, and form to everything that it experiences and stores in memory.

It acts through that limited knowledge, which is what we use. If you tell the mind to stop playing that movie, then the limited perception will stop. You will see everything as fact without any naming or preconceived opinion or judgment. You will become one with it and will start to experience what joy and bliss are. The first time I understand the Pathway for direct perception.

Get control over your mind and shut it up. Know it's nature to find past evidence from memory and give you all sorts of thoughts. Tell that mind I don't need it. Thank you. Now it is up to us to practice yoga meditation to get to that level.

So, buckle up, baby. Let us go on the roller coaster ride of Disneyland of our own inner consciousness. If we can do it, anything is possible. The joy and bliss we are, are ours to experience. What is happening to our body and mind is a part of our consciousness, awareness.

If we get control over the mind and get into the realm of consciousness, body and mind obey, and there will be no ailment. I never truly believed until now, so all the spiritual reading was futile. Now I feel I have direction.

So, buckle up. We are on a flight of our new life beyond these worldly pleasures and pains!

34.   INHALE INHALE.

3/21/22

You still cannot see a word and recognize it even though you know it and you spell it. You struggle to read each letter. You struggle to make a sentence from each word. Your brain is not pulling the verbs associated with the word.

My logical mind is giving me ample evidence to doubt full recovery and pull me down the dark alley of depression. Thank God I have this other spiritual knowledge to wipe the darkness with light. I can tell that small mind to shut up and

bring it to the self where the powerplant is. It should always have energy; however strong the obstacles may be. Identification with the body-mind occurs but only sticks for a short time. Yesterday our yoga guru tried to give me that evidence.

The yoga teacher wanted me to sit on the floor and get up without support. "There is no way I could", I told her based on experience even from the day before yesterday. She kept saying, inhale inhale and I could do both sit up and down without support.

She convinced me if the mind believes, it happens. Your teacher told you it is the confidence you need to have, that your mind is far more powerful. My left rotator cuff tear needs surgery. I told her I needed my deltoid strong. She did so many more advanced shoulder yoga, it baffled me.

I doubted her confidence and thought that she was going to exaggerate my problem, making it from a small to a big tear. My resistance was to the utmost When it came to actions that I knew would cause me pain. She said to focus on the waist where you are bending, not the stretch on your shoulder. When I did that, the shoulder stretched without pain, to my surprise. She said now you know your mind was getting in the way.

Convinced I was yesterday that the mind is far more powerful. Taru reads Sadguru book telling how to get that power each one has. Your three parts, body, mind, emotions, and energy, have to be aligned. There are yogic processes for each. Anyone can do it.

He says there are two parts to us that most people don't recognize. The body and mind for survival mode that keeps us grounded in emergencies, and the second part is grace that tries to lift us up constantly. When we try to mix them up, conflict

arises. If we know they are separate, then body does its work and grace does it's. So now we know where we are going wrong. So I am convinced we focus on the side of grace; fully, your aphasia will take care of itself. We make sure 100% action on speech therapy is not faulted on your side.

My quantum healing book talked about how when focusing on the positive ability of your mind, the energy flows to all million regenerating cells every day and quantum healing occurs. Your immune cells are the receivers of these healing messages from your mind along with your brain. We are attacking your aphasia from every angle.

S We are 71. Our window of achieving that higher consciousness is short. On the other hand, we are retired and have all the time in our hands. We have an incentive for you to get better, to prove to science how restricted the current science is. Our lack of desire for travel, parties, the worldly jazz is our fuel. So let us fuel the rocket and launch into our adventure!

35.   ILLUSION

3/22/22

Your diplopia is getting worse. That would mean there is an active lesion in the brainstem, perhaps! So logically, at the body level, we should plan to go back to Houston for a repeat MRI and possible infusion. I made a reservation at the

Marriott Hotel rotary house connected to the hospital. I could only get three nights there. We will stay with Viren and Danielle for the rest of the four days. I want to avoid dealing with Airbnb or VRBO and rental cars. Too many unnecessary additions create stress.

At the mind level, there is initial resistance as I do not want active PML to be the outcome. Why? What are the tricks this mind is playing? The mind expresses insecurity, fear of morbidity and mortality, or fear of loss.

Glad I heard swami TV's lecture today.

How come the lecture of the day is the solution for that day's problem? I wonder. But he talked about adhyaas, the illusion. The rope looks like a serpent in the dark, but the presumed serpent is a rope in the light. So is the world we see in waking state as it goes away in sleep.

His explanation is, and you see if it makes sense. If you have a wand with a glow at its end, you twirl it and write I love you in the air, is I love you there? Similarly, the reflection of atma, the light that we are, when reflected in the conditioned consciousness, the movement of which creates the I love you of that glow called the world. The space is a circle, and time is the frequency. This consciousness is the mind. When there is movement in the mind, the mind is agitated; the illusion is created that creates attachment and

aversion, the real cause of suffering. When the mind is quiet, there is no movement like in still water, you can see the sun, you can see the true nature of unlimited you in the quiet mind. So let us apply this to our situation.

The fear of PML relapsing, you suffering and dying, me not being able to let go of attachment to you is all adhyas. I would say any insecurity is adhyaas. Then why the suffering? Make sure we pass this exam with flying colors. Let us see the facts.

Let us abide in our true self, the powerful peaceful, joyous us, irrespective of what happens to the limited body. This high energy will be able to heal the sick cells as each cell has intelligence, and they are bathing in intelligence all around them.

Do not lose our focus. We can keep that mind free of unnecessary movements and access our power. Body and death are adhyas that are bound to go one day as they are impermanent. So let us be like our yoga teacher said yesterday.

In spite of the chaos around us, our minds should be always quite peaceful, and joyful. So let us be that. Do not let the mind take over us; let us tame that mind and enjoy our joy.

36.   NEW OMICRON VARIANT, NEW WAVE AGAIN!

3/23/22

Just when I thought I am on top of everything, the hotel booked, informed the nurse when we wanted to come, another bomb shell! The questions are getting tougher in our exam of life. Need to focus even harder.

I read the article last night omicron new variant BA2 is here in NY, NJ. New Hampshire. It has peaked in London. They have learned that it is far more contagious than omicron, almost equating to measles. One infected person will spread it to 8 others.

The peak in USA will be at the end of March, and we will travel on 31st of March. Even though it is similar to morbidity and mortality as omicron for vaccinated people, for immune-compromised, both are quite high. With such rampant spread

and with the new mask-free environment, traveling and escaping getting infected can't coexist. So quick reaction would be omg. But let us respond not react. Avoiding travel would be best. Let us repeat MRI here. If there is no activity we can stay here.

If symptoms continue to get worse, we got to go. In that case, leave now before the spread and stay in Houston. Cancel the hotel. Stay with Danielle. She is insisting we stay with her. It is good for her morale. She is going through so much and feels comforted when we are there. They are happy when we are there, and you are happy to be with their dog Amber. But if the infusion is not needed, why travel? We don't have much time.

I need to make a decision. Let us see what the doctor says.

If it makes sense, buying or renting a house in Houston may not be a bad idea. Staying in Phoenix is like we are nowhere, neither in LA nor Houston. Your speech therapist is so good, leaving her would be tough, and getting a new appointment for speech therapy in Houston takes time means you will be without therapy again. I know how important speech therapy is for you. Let's prepare to take off in case we have to.

How do we keep this mind calm? Let me share what I learned this morning. I am not sure how to apply it to our situation. It said the instrument with the glow when moves, writes I love you and the information gets stored in the mind even if it is not real.

Next time, when needed, it pulls that information out and makes you believe that it is real. That is a universal belief that rope is the serpent. But if you use the instrument and shed light on it you can see the truth. We will have to keep an open mind because mind wants to resist, saying it is bull shit.

Another instrument a spectrophotometer, can see the frequencies of light and can tell what the thing is. You test necklace, bracelet, ring, anklet any ornament with it, it will say it is gold. The gold is the truth, the base substrate.

Similar instrument in our life is our intellect called buddhi. Right intellect will see gold in the ornaments. The wrong intellect will see ornaments. The name and form. Our right intellect should be able to see brahman or the divine energy as substratum or truth behind the mind, body, tree animal, etc.

Be cognizant of the superimposition, focusing on who we truly are, the fear of what happens to the body that is illusory should go away. This is all against logical thinking but if want to experiment, we have to experiment just as prescribed, then say it is right or wrong. I truly feel we will be guided if we keep that mind calm.

We keep giving our 100% in actions that are needed, but the middle layer, the mind, keep control over it. I don't feel anxious. Let us not be afraid of the unknown. Sadguru says only bold people are comfortable with unknown and unknown is where the Magical and Spark of life lies.

The unlimited boundless knowingness and joy lie in unknown. So let us be the witness of what happens next in our life with a cool mind.

37.   NEW MYSTERY DIPLOPIA

3/26/22

Thought of traveling on Thursday to Houston, but the first-class ticket was $3000 per person product of the Russia war, Covid, spring break, and greedy businesses trying to make up for their losses. Wonder ever the thought surfaces to their hardened mind, what source does the hiked-up airfare come from?

Ordinary people or health compromised who will pay any price to save life. Maybe they don't, as money-making goal puts blinders on the sides of their eyes like they do on horses.

How can anyone with a conscience use that money without hurting your conscience? Can greed drain humanity to a level that no drop of compassion is left in the heart? Sometimes you are faced with forcing the wrong behavior because Job demands it but check with your heart. Doctors of this era are faced with the same dilemma.

Work for corporations and do what they want you to do, make money. From whom, ordinary people who barely can make ends meet. Don't do enough procedures, can't make money. I have seen doctor friends fired as they didn't meet the quota. Lack of time with the patient is the tool used to make more money.

I changed my practice when the choice for survival was to do more procedures indicated or no, even though you can twist your words in the chart so the insurance sees a justification. For me protecting my conscience was a priority. But how can most young doctors fight the Goliath?

Won't it be an experiment to make the rule makers actually go through the experience of going through the health system, pay as charged, see the bills, similar to the actual patients?

Then those with still some conscience alive, may wake up. Or is it that compassion is not taught anymore when you are a child? So, we are going to Houston next week. Your diplopia is slightly increasing. Mystery again to be solved as you are so unique.

Is it due to PML? Do you need another infusion? Extra infusions don't come without a risk of rejecting your lung. I talked with Dr Olson yesterday. She is puzzled. Out of 25 patients, no one has relapsed. She thought you were over it.

She says you are a unique case. We will repeat MRI and CSF and probably do one more infusion. I hope you don't need it. We need a second opinion from Neuro ophthalmology. Maybe your diplopia is due to something else. Let us do one more trip.

I still see my mind feeling a sense of disappointment, sadness, and pain. I thought we were out of danger. How he talks about pain and pleasure in his morning talk today. Glad I have this psychotherapy, as I am still waiting for

Psychologist's appointment for the past four months, who will take my insurance. Isn't it strange we have three insurances good ones but because we are over 65, government makes us make Medicare our primary, which pays less. Many doctors don't take it for that reason. But if they don't take Medicare, even though we have two other top-of-the-line insurances, doctors are not allowed to bill them.

So, they can't see us. It is like having thousands of dollars in your pocket. But is like a foreign currency that can't be exchanged. Now I know how people on Medicaid must be feeling. No one wants to see them as the insurance pays so little. These are the same people with two arms two legs and a head, mind and emotions like us, but they can't get good medical treatment because they are poor for some reason or the other.

So let me tell you what I learned today how to rise above pain and pleasure because I sure need it today.

The reasons why you want a change, may be job, friend, relationship, partner, house, vacation is because you are not content with what you have; because you are unhappy and not full. Desire to change equates to the absence of contentment.

No amount of change is going to get you that happiness. So instead of wandering all your life, from one thing to the other, rise above the 6 waves that come in your life. Learn to surf these waves, and you notice you have a fountain of joy.

The first and second are birth and death. Pain occurs because you are so mind-body identified. We are so conditioned from childhood; we believe it. No question asked. Go deeper, and you will notice that belief is like a grove. Like a tram will only

Go in a grove. It cannot go around freely like a car. Our identification with the body is like that tram in a grove of the belief that I am the body. Every cognition, every thought is associated with the light of awareness, but we ignore that and think the body is me.

The body is created in the mind, and you are the witness of the mind. So, focus on examining your mind and you won't identify with the mind and body. Then there is no question of pain and pleasure happening to you.

Second wave to get over is pain and pleasure. Pain occurs when you are not content with what you have. You compare yourself with other and want what they have. Even if you get it you will find another who has more. You will never be happy.

You have to cultivate contentment. Anything more than necessary for the survival of life, food, clothing, and shelter is excessive. When you desire and obtain more the temporary pleasure contains in it longer term pain. Desire makes you slave.

Once you know you are the source of joy, then why go after material things to get joy which eventually derived from you anyway, then why not take over the warehouse of joy? Learn the techniques to tap into joy which you are, on demand.

Third wave is hunger and thirst. Eat when naturally hungry and thirsty. Emotional eating, eating for enjoyment is a sign you are a slave to hunger and thirst.

Rise above it. You will know you will easily tap into your joy if you rise above this wave.

So, let us consciously watch the body and mind, watch the show and rise above the wave of pain and pleasure as we are the source of joy; why are we looking for pleasure in the desire of healing? Mind will take care of healing the body. Let's not disturb it.

Let's bathe in the joy that we are.

38.   WOMEN'S GROUP STARTED!

3/27/22

I went for the picnic our Antakshri group hosted for Women's Day. In the backdrop of reddish-brown mountains with literally the holes in them, we met in ramada 14 picnic spot. Usha from our group had arrived earlier, so did Sushama, and Uma from our group.

Our Antakshri group was born as a result of filling the gap of loneliness in 5 random ladies who had one thing in common, love for singing. Usha not highly educated, coming from a small town in Haryana, but the smartest and most courageous with the entrepreneur mindset, and the successful comedian took it upon herself to organize, pick up pizza, and water bottles and set up the picnic tables.

One by one, ladies started arriving, all unknown to each other, in varied sizes, shapes, age, professions and most of all personalities. Name tags bypassed the pressure of trying to remember the names. Pizza, chips, sweets, and tangerines were enough to bind all of us. Younger ones brought their young ones. Some three generations also mingled.

Hobbies part of the introductions started forming future groups organically. Cooking surfaced at the top, gardening next then few rare ones like sewing, reading etc. Many got interested in my idea of the book by the next women's day about collecting experiences of these varied women on how life is in USA and what they can teach others through their experiences.

There were oldies who had immigrated 40-50 years ago; some got divorced at age 50, some at 70, some wanting to divorce but couldn't do it, some happily married, one with white American husband, one came from India and married Indian born and raised in America. Issues to me were would a person Indian looking but born and brought up in USA relate better to an American than an Indian coming from India?

Are the skin colors or the culture more important for successful cohabitation? I surely want to have these two women's stories in my book. The younger Indian woman freshly coming from India more westernized, trying to assimilate, will be a good contrast to the older ones not as westernized. The shyness of the youngest, the assertiveness of the little older and the holding on the Indian culture talk of the older one created a flavorful soup.

We decided to write about the experiences and resources for the survival and progress of a single Indian woman in the USA. Each woman will have achieved one goal of their choice by the next women's day.

Others promised to help Vrushali distribute food for homeless. This was followed by games, songs, dance. Not a bad start for our spur-of-the-moment idea to meet for women's day.

39. GAMBLER OF LIFE, WIN OVER THE VIRUS.

4/7/22

We are back from Houston

Everything stable on your MRI

Hopefully this is the end of the chapter of PML in our life. What a roller coaster ride! beats Disneyland. It is the ride of our minds that is both frightening as well as exhilarating!

Now the second ride of our life starts, living with a speech disability. It is a new terrain for us and others. It is like a new life has started, and we are in the first grade. Learning to deal with new challenges, changing social landscape.

It is like creating a new life, akin to making a delicious dish from restricted ingredients. Your grit, persistence, courage and overpouring love will make this life even more beautiful and meaningful. You are lucky god forgot to put the gene of negativity in your DNA.

As if someone is guiding us, today's reading gave a guideline to make a beautiful life possible. Remember, nobody can harm us, only we can harm ourselves. So, hostility and feuds will automatically stop. That makes loving everybody easier.

Let us be simple and single. Mind not wanting things will make us simple and avoid traps of disappointments in our life. Let us be single, live in humanity but single, alone but not lonely. Let us watch situations to come in our life as a movie

But stay detached from them like the light in the projector. Let us stop labeling the situations and people, good or bad, pleasant or painful. One follows the other without a doubt. These feelings happen in the mind anyway. We have total control over it.

A gambler wants to keep winning. He is happy when he wins. He is painfully hurt when he loses. We all do the same in life. So let us remember the gambler when things go wrong. Let us accept every situation as is and not become a gambler of our life.

Stop identifying with the mind like the movie and we will rise above. Our true unlimited creativity will reveal. Our self is a power plant full of energy no matter how hard is the obstacle. That is it. This is the formula.

We were at the top of the class in medical school. We can do the same in school of this life. So let us buckle up and start the romance with life, the ride this time, instead of a roller coaster, will be a cruise, slow steady, and fun. We invite anyone who wants, to join the cruise of our life.

ACKNOWLEDGEMENT

My great thanks to Dilip, my husband for letting me share his story. Even though personal and being vulnerable, he wanted to help others by sharing what we went through in the process of our journey. Thanks to my children for helping me create this book. Thanks to Alka Joshi for sharing her knowledge and Jayna Clerk for sharing her experience. Thank you Suresh for formatting the book.

ABOUT THE AUTHOR

Dr. Smita Kittur

Smita Kittur is a neurologist, born in India, a writer, trained at Johns Hopkins Hospital. Dr. Kittur has done research in area of memory disorders, anxiety and depression. She has interest in applying spiritual and non medical methods for treating anxiety and depression. She has published short stories in Art Inscribed and had readings at Laguna beach art festival. Her poems are read at shows and has gotten inspiring reviews. She also is an artist and a pilot. She is interested in sharing her medical experience in her writings.